8x 4/56   24x 5.

DATE

The Let's Talk Library™

Let's Talk About
Feeling Defeated

Melanie Ann Apel

The Rosen Publishing Group's
PowerKids Press™
New York

To Lisa Tolnai. The best. The very best! Love, Melanie

Published in 2002 by The Rosen Publishing Group, Inc.
29 East 21st Street, New York, NY 10010

First Edition

Book Design: Emily Muschinske

Project Editors: Jennifer Landau, Jason Moring, Jennifer Quasha

Photo Credits: p. 4 by Joseph Muschinske; p. 7 © Owen Franken/CORBIS; p. 8 © Kevin Fleming/CORBIS; p. 11 © Jim Sugar Photography/CORBIS; p. 12 © Richard T. Nowitz/CORBIS; p. 15 © Image Bank/L D Gordon; pp. 16, 19 © CORBIS; p. 20 © Jennie Woodcock; Reflections PhotoLibrary/CORBIS.

Apel, Melanie Ann.
Let's talk about feeling defeated / Melanie Ann Apel.
  p. cm. — (The let's talk about library)
Includes index.
  ISBN 0–8239–5864–7 (lib. bdg.)
1. Emotions in children–Juvenile literature. 2. Defeat (Psychology)–Juvenile literature. [1. Emotions. 2. Defeat (Psychology)] I. Title. II. Series.
  BF723.E6 .A74 2001
  152.4—dc21

00–012193

Manufactured in the United States of America

Contents

Melissa and Noah

Melissa and Noah are on a soccer team. The team practices twice a week. They have a game every Saturday. Melissa and Noah have lost their last two games. They and their team are feeling **defeated**. Even though Melissa and Noah have been practicing hard and doing all of their soccer drills, their team keeps losing. This makes them feel **frustrated** and sad.

◀ *Losing a game can make us feel bad.*

Defining Defeat

The word defeat means to lose a contest, a battle, or a game. It also means to stop feeling hopeful for something. You may have heard the word undefeated. To be undefeated means never to lose. The word defeat is often **associated** with sports. For example, if your sports team never lost a game, they were undefeated. People can feel defeated at other times, too.

When things are not going well in our lives, we can feel defeated. ▶

Who Feels Defeated?

Have you ever tried very hard to do something special? For example, you may have practiced a lot for the school concert, but played a wrong note anyway. Perhaps you studied hard for a test, but you didn't get the grade that you wanted. How did you feel? You probably felt sad and angry. Maybe you thought that all of your hard work was for nothing. You may have felt like you would never get anything right. This is feeling defeated. Everyone feels defeated at one time or another. You are not alone.

At times, it seems that no matter how hard we try things just don't work out.

When Everything Goes Wrong

Brady had a really bad day. She forgot to feed her goldfish before school. She left her lunch box on the kitchen counter. Even though she studied hard for her math test, she doesn't think she did very well. On the school trip, Brady didn't get to share a canoe with her best friend, Jason. When Brady got home, a note from her father told her to clean her room again. He didn't think she did a good job yesterday. "I just can't do anything right," Brady thinks. Brady is feeling defeated.

When many problems happen all at once, we may feel like things will never be good again. ▶

Step Back and Start Again

When you are feeling defeated, it can be hard to pick yourself up and start over again. But you can do it! Think about all of the things you do well. Ask yourself whether or not you really tried your hardest. If you did not try your hardest, know that you can do better the next time. Even when we try to do the best we can, things still may not work out the way we want them to. When you are feeling defeated, you may want to talk to an adult you trust, such as your mother or father, your teacher, or your coach.

◀ *The people who succeed are those who keep trying, even if sometimes they feel defeated.*

It's Okay to Lose

You usually feel defeated because you lose at something or do not do as well as you would like. It is important to remember that you can't be the winner all of the time. Sometimes the other team or the better speller will win. Sometimes, no matter how much you practice your instrument, someone with more experience still will give a better **performance** than you. This is okay. If you always won, then everyone else always would feel defeated. Sometimes you are the winner, other times you are not. You can get used to not winning every time.

It's easy to feel good when we win, but it is important to feel good when we try hard and lose anyway. ▶

Losing Gracefully

David played against his friend Alex in baseball. Alex's team won by eight runs. David got mad. He thought Alex's team cheated. David didn't understand that Alex won because he was lucky. If you learn how to lose **gracefully**, you will feel better. Losing gracefully means understanding that no matter how hard you try, sometimes the other person or the other team still will do better. Try to **congratulate** the winner rather than feeling sorry for yourself. You will feel stronger when you do this.

◀ *When we congratulate others, we are a part of their victory. This can keep us from feeling defeated.*

Did You Really Try?

Emily did not do well on her swimming test. She was **embarrassed** when she told her mother how she did. She felt defeated because she had thought she would do better. Emily's coach asked her how much she had practiced. Emily **confessed** that she had practiced only a few times. Emily's coach pointed out that if Emily had practiced more, she might have done better. The next time, her coach helped her practice, and Emily passed with the highest score!

People can do amazing things, but we won't know what we can do until we really try our best. ▶

Getting Help

When Joey's mom brought his baby sister home, Joey was **jealous**. Joey's mom was busy with the new baby. Joey felt defeated because no matter what he did, he could not get his mother's attention. Joey's big brother Max helped him. Max told Joey that he had felt the same way when Joey was born. Max reminded Joey that he was a big brother. Everyone would need Joey to help with the new baby. Max also told Joey that their little sister needed him, too. This made Joey feel much better.

Feeling defeated can make us feel unwanted. No matter how bad we feel, though, there is always someone who can help us to cheer up.

Things Do Work Out

   Torrie and Liza spent the afternoon making cupcakes for their dad's birthday. They left the cupcakes to cool and went outside to play. When they came back inside to frost the cupcakes, they found only a few crumbs on the table and on their dog Bingo! Liza started to cry because she felt tired and defeated. Torrie felt differently. She started to laugh because she thought it was funny. Torrie suggested that they quickly bake a cake for their dad. Torrie's idea helped Lisa stop feeling defeated. Then the idea of Bingo eating all of the cupcakes made her laugh!

Glossary

associated (uh-SOH-see-ay-ted) Having to do with.

confessed (kun-FEST) Told the truth about something that you did wrong.

congratulate (kun-GRA-joo-layt) To tell someone you are proud of something that he or she did.

defeated (dih-FEE-ted) Losing a contest or a battle or a game; to feel as if nothing is going right.

embarrassed (im-BAYR-ist) Feeling uncomfortable or ashamed.

frustrated (FRUS-tray-ted) Feeling angry or sad because you cannot do anything about a certain situation.

gracefully (GRAYS-fuh-lee) Politely or kindly.

jealous (JEL-us) To want what someone else has.

performance (per-FOR-muns) A public entertainment.

Index